The
SET AND FORGET
11% Portfolio

A Low Risk ETF Investing Strategy That Averages Over 11% Annually and Requires Just 4 Trades a Year

By Tim Morris

Copyright © 2019
All Rights Reserved.
ISBN: 9781710997996
Published by ZML Corp LLC

Table of Contents

Disclaimer

This book is for entertainment and informational purposes only. By purchasing this book, you agree to not give any of the strategy presented in this book away in the review section of Amazon. Any reviews with information related to this strategy will be reported to Amazon and deleted.

The creator of this book is not an investment advisory service, a registered investment advisor, or a broker-dealer and does not advise clients on which securities they should buy or sell for themselves. It must be understood that a very high degree of risk is involved in trading stocks. The publisher of this book, and the affiliates of the publisher assume no responsibility or liability for trading and investment results. It should not be assumed that the methods, techniques, or indicators presented in this book will be profitable nor that they will not result in losses. In addition, the indicators, strategies, rules and all other features of the information presented are provided for information and educational purposes only and should not be construed as investment advice.

Investors and traders must always consult with their licensed financial advisors and tax advisors before partaking in any investment. The author and publisher have no affiliation with any brokers or websites listed in this book. The author receives compensation for the affiliate links used in the book. Copyright © 2019, all rights reserved. Written by Tim Morris. Published by ZML Corp LLC.

About the Author

Hello there! My name is Tim Morris and I've been trading stocks for many years. I originally got into the stock market when my grandfather set up a $3,000 Charles Schwab account for me when I was 5 years old, and I haven't looked back since. My general philosophy is to use the stock market as a long term tool for wealth. While you can of course day trade, swing trade, etc., it's best to do this with funds you can afford to lose, and long term gains should be your main goal when investing.

For most people, using the stock market as a long term investment vehicle is what will allow you to build wealth. I want you to think of the future, not a get rich quick scheme. I can't tell you how many times I kick myself thinking "if I would have just left my money in something safe years ago I'd have so much more now." As you may have attempted yourself, I tried all the get rich quick schemes when I was young and... surprise, surprise... they didn't work.

If you have a full time job, and you're able to be frugal and save a large portion of each paycheck you get, just think of what 11% a year can do for you. In 10 years, you'll have built up a fortune that you can use. You can put it into your retirement, buy a home, go on vacation, or anything else you want.

If you'd like to learn more about me, as well as view informative articles I have written and see more of my books, go to my website at TradeMoreStocks.com.

Also I want to point out why this book is so large. This book measures 8.25" x 8.25". I started out with a much smaller paperback version at 5" x 8", however the many charts I have throughout the book were barely visible. So I had to make the book larger to give the reader a better visual on the charts.

> **NOTE:** As stated in the disclaimer, even if for some reason you don't like this book, do not place any of this strategy in the review section of Amazon or you will have your account reported to Amazon and have your review deleted. Thank you.

Introduction

In this book, we will be going over an incredibly efficient, low-risk stock investment strategy. This is a long-term, buy and hold strategy that is meant to be held indefinitely. This strategy is perfect for those who are risk-adverse, those entering retirement age, those who don't like constantly checking their portfolio every day, or anyone else who wants to both beat inflation and grow their wealth in a safe way. When sticking to the rules provided in this book, you can expect to earn an average return of over 11% a year.

Understand this is an average. Some years it will be more, some years it will be less. However, based on back testing of the last 32 years, even during recessions, this strategy has never gone down more than 4% in any given year. Compare this to the S&P 500 which has gone down over 37%, and you can see the benefits of this strategy. Having to worry about if and when losses will happen in your account is tough. It eats most traders up. This strategy comes very close to eliminating that.

This book was written in a way so it is easy to understand for everyone, which would include new or novice investors. If you are more experienced, you may be aware of some of the items I bring up, however the main strategy I present later on will still be the ultimate value of this book. So without further ado, let's learn about *The Set & Forget Portfolio.*

Chapter 1
Key Information

In this chapter I will be going over items which are necessary to know while reading this book. Some of this may be common knowledge to you however I still advise you to read this chapter as you may learn a few things.

S&P 500

First we need to talk about the S&P 500. In the United States, the Standard & Poor's 500 is a market index which tracks the 500 largest companies in the stock market listed on the New York and NASDAQ stock exchanges. Generally the S&P 500 is referenced when people are talking about the stock market. For example, when someone says "how's the market doing," they are most likely referring to if the S&P 500 is up or down on the day.

Treasury Bonds

Treasury bonds are certificates issued from the government. I'll be referring to the

United States government in this book, however most countries around the world issue treasury bonds in their own currency, and the information in this book can be applied to other countries as well.

Treasury bonds range in length from 1 month to 30 years (with 50 year and 100 year bonds possibly being released in the future). Meaning the government gets to keep your money for the length of time you choose, and you receive interest on your money while they hold it. Generally a larger percentage of interest is paid on longer term bonds. At the time of writing this book, the US government currently pays annual bond yields which fall between 1.58% - 2.21%.

Bonds do not make as much money as stocks, but are considered a "safe-haven" because you are guaranteed money from the government. Investors usually rush into treasury bonds during downturns in the stock market because treasury bonds are "safe." While investors are only making 1%-2% a year in treasury bonds, they would be losing money holding stocks during these recessionary time periods.

CAGR

When you hear someone talk about a portfolio or investment strategy, they will usually reference the CAGR, which is an abbreviation for the **compound annual growth rate**. This is just the average amount received annually from an investment portfolio over a specified time frame. So, for example, let's say you have money in a stock for a 2 year time frame. During the first year the stock increases in price by 10%. During the second year, it increases by 20%. Over that two year time period, your CAGR would calculated out to be 15%.

Mutual Funds & ETFs

While consumers could invest in stocks individually, it can become time consuming and a hassle to manage a large number of stocks in your portfolio. Companies understood this and came out with what are called mutual funds. These are funds you buy with your broker, which end in the letter "X", and are actually a combination of many different stocks into one "symbol." An example of a mutual fund by the popular company Vanguard, is the Vanguard 500 Index Fund with ticker symbol VFINX. Mutual funds come with management fees, which are fees charged to investors by the company who runs the mutual fund. Investors who have their money in mutual funds must pay these fees. Mutual funds also typically require a minimum dollar amount and do not trade like regular stocks, but instead can only be bought/sold at the end of the trading day.

In the early 1990's, exchange traded funds (ETFs) made their debut. These are essentially mutual funds with ticker symbols which can be bought and sold like regular stocks. They also usually have lower management fees, called expense ratios, and do not require any type of minimum dollar amount to get started. As such, they have become much more popular than mutual funds. An example of a very popular ETF is SPY, which is an ETF which correlates with the S&P 500, and is run by a company called State Street Global Advisors.

Dividends

Dividends are essentially checks issued to shareholders of a stock each quarter. Not all companies issue dividends, and for the ones that do, the amount can vary widely. Let me go over a quick example.

Stock XYZ yields a 4% dividend, and you own $100 worth of stock XYZ. The 4% dividend is the annual percentage received, meaning each quarter you would receive 1/4th of this from the company. So after one quarter, you would receive 1% of the total stock you own in the form of a dividend check, making your account balance now worth $101 (granted the stock price didn't change in this fictional scenario). And at the end of the year, you'd have received all four quarterly dividend checks. This means the total 4% dividend, or $4 in this case, would be in your account, making your account balance now worth $104.

There are a variety of reasons companies issue dividends, but you could think of them like interest on a bond. As in the company is paying you for the time you are leaving your money in their stock. I bring up dividends because the ETFs we will be going over in this book issue dividends, which end up increasing the annual return you receive each year.

Inflation

If you were to earn money from a job and put it under your mattress, it would decrease in value over time. This is due to inflation, which is an issue with any fiat (governmental) currency. This is because most governments are not on any type of "gold standard" and can print money at will (which they love doing). This in turn devalues the currency and leads to inflation. Since 1914, the US inflation rate has averaged 3.22% a year. Considering this, something that costs $1 today will cost $1.03 next year. If you do the math, this means in 20 years, prices have doubled due to inflation. This is the reason why investors put their money in stocks and bonds, in an effort to both beat inflation and increase the value of their stationary money.

Drawdowns & Annual Returns

As I will use the word in this book, a **drawdown** is considered the amount a stock or bond has decreased in a given time frame from its highest point to its lowest point. That time frame can range from multiple months to multiple years, depending on where the highest and lowest points are.

For example, let's say a stock is valued at $100 on January 1st. In March of the same year, that stock rises to $110, which is the highest point it reaches all year. In August, that stock decreases in price to $90, which is the lowest point it reached all year. That stock had a max-drawdown of -18.18%.

On December 31st, this same stock closes at $95. While it had a -18.18% max drawdown back in August, considering it closed at $95 at the end of the year, it had an **annual return** of -5%. This is because it started the year at $100, and closed the year at $95. (100-95=5, 5/100 = -5%)

Sharpe & Sortino Ratios

In an effort to better understand the risk/reward correlated with stock portfolios, professionals have come up with ratios which give data in numerical form. Two very common ratios are the Sharpe ratio and Sortino ratio, with a higher number correlating to a better investment for both. Sharpe and Sortino ratios are calculated slightly differently, with the Sortino ratio putting no weight on upside volatility.

I happen to think the Sortino ratio is more relevant, considering I don't really mind if there is volatility on the way up, since I'm still making money. In essence though, both take into account the amount made over a given time period versus the amount lost, as well as the volatility experienced, and give you a number which reflects how beneficial of an investment a portfolio was.

The items I just went over should provide you with all the background information necessary to accurately understand the rest of this book. To use the strategy I will be going over, you first need to understand the reason why it works. Because of this, I will now be going over the relationship between the two items we will be keeping in our portfolio, which are stocks and bonds.

Chapter 2
Stocks

If you live in a country other than the United States, a similar strategy will be effective in your country. I go over more information regarding this in Chapter 5. Read the whole book first though to understand how this strategy works.

When most people think of investing in the stock market, they think of stocks. As in companies they can buy which will hopefully increase in price and make them money in the long run. As you may have found, trying to pick a stock in the hope it will rise can be a tough prospect. There are currently around 3,500 stocks listed in US stock market. Which one do you pick? There are competing theories in regards to how to pick a stock with fundamental, technical, and quantitative analysis being the most commonly referenced. Mastering any of these can take a bit of time, however most would argue all three are necessary to be successful. And even if you are to pick a "correct" stock which rises in price through the years, there will most likely have been another that would have risen more. Not to mention the fact the general market could have easily beaten the stock(s) you picked.

This leads to the next fact which is since the early 1900's, the S&P 500 has averaged over 9% in annual returns, as in it has a CAGR of over 9%. Meaning if you were to invest in the S&P 500, over the long run, you would make over 9% a year.

I would argue that, for most traders, trying to pick individual stocks and make your own portfolio ends up being more of a hassle than it's worth. As I talk about in my free special report *Crush the Market*, over 95% of hedge funds do not beat the S&P 500. You could compare a hedge fund to a financial advisor, except they are financial advisors for people with a lot of money. Many hedge funds have very high entrance requirements, in the hundreds of thousands of dollars, meaning they are managing millions and billions of dollars worth of money. As such, they are able to hire the best and brightest financial experts, many of whom have graduated from Ivy League schools like Harvard and Yale. Yet still, 95% of these hedge funds do not beat the S&P 500 each year! So why would the everyday trader think they can do better? It's more beneficial to just use the general market's known gains as your backbone.

The issue we come across when investing in the general market is volatility. Let me show you a chart of the S&P 500 from the 1980's to the present day. All the charts in this book **start with $10,000**, adding nothing to them along the way. They also all start in 1987 and end in 2019, showing you **32 years of history**. I feel this is plenty of historical data to prove the strategy I will be going over in this book. The chart below shows the mutual fund VFINX, which is a Vanguard mutual fund which correlates with the S&P 500.

100% Stocks

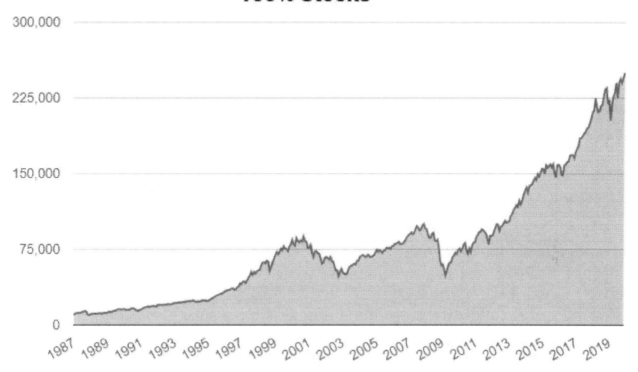

Stats

Allocation:	100% VFINX
Initial Balance:	$10,000
Final Balance:	$250,111
CAGR:	10.30%
Max Drawdown:	-50.97%
Worst Year:	-37.02%
Sharpe Ratio:	0.54
Sortino Ratio:	0.77

This means if you had invested just $10,000 in the SP500 in 1987, you would have over $250,000 in your stock account today. The issue is we aren't hibernated in a cave for 30 years and are engrossed in the present day. While 10.30% a year is an excellent return greatly beating inflation, it's hard for many traders to take the kind of drawdowns associated with this strategy. I hate seeing my stock account lose a few hundred dollars, not to mention thousands. Let's go over what those drawdowns and annual returns would have looked like.

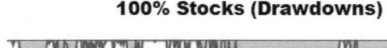

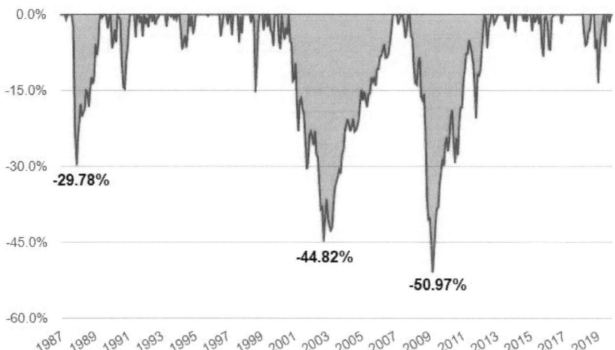

100% Stocks (Annual Returns)

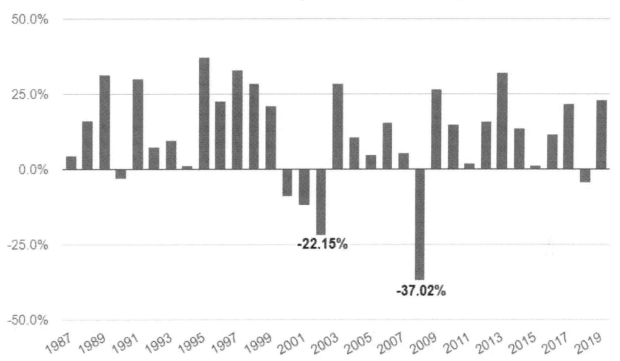

As you see from the charts, you would have been partying all night in 2000 when your account rose to over $135,000, however less than two years later it would have sunk over 44%. Losses like this can be very hard to deal with for investors. Not only that, you really can't touch your money during this time period because you need it to recover, which can of course take many years to happen. What if you need the money now though?

The same thing then happened again in 2008, and the crash at that time was even worse, having a max drawdown of over 50%. Talk about a tough time to be in stocks! While it's understood the market will eventually move higher after a crash, you don't know when. Losses like this are very hard to stomach for most people. Investors are aware of this which is why they buy bonds.

Chapter 3
Treasury Bonds

There are many types of bonds, however we will be focusing on long term treasury bonds in this book. Bonds can be issued from both governments and companies. Treasury bonds are issued from the government, specifically the United States government in this book. How it works is you give the government your money, and they guarantee you a percentage yield each year. For example, if you were to give the government $20,000 for a bond yielding 2.5%, you would earn $500 a year while the government holds your money. Typically higher yields are offered for longer term bonds. Meaning if you put your money in a 1 year bond, the US government will offer you a lower annual percentage yield than if you had invested in a 30 year bond. The definition of a long term treasury bond is twenty years or greater.

Treasury bonds are considered a very safe investment because unlike a company, they are backed by the United States government which is unlikely to go "out of business" in the future. This means you are all but guaranteed to get your percentage yield each year.

Fortunately for us, there are many ETFs which mimic bonds that we can buy with our general broker as opposed to physically buying a bond. These ETFs go up and down with bond rates, and generally perform better over the long term versus buying an actual bond. Let's look at how the Vanguard long term treasury bond mutual fund, VUSTX, has done over the last 32 years.

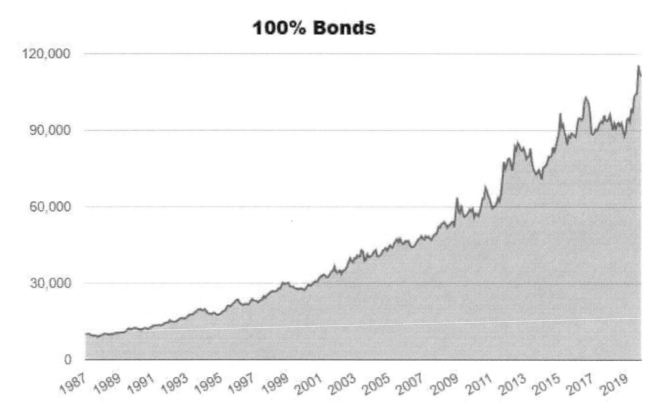

100% Bonds

100% Bonds (Annual Returns)

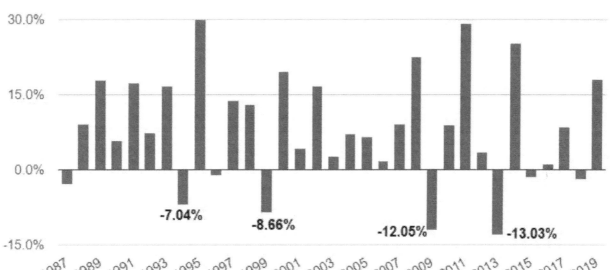

Stats

Allocation:	100% VUSTX
Initial Balance:	$10,000
Ending Balance:	$111,370
CAGR:	7.62%
Max Drawdown:	-16.68%
Worst Year:	-13.03%
Sharpe Ratio:	0.49
Sortino Ratio:	0.81

As you can see, investing in bonds is less volatile than purely investing in stocks, however it does not have the same amount of growth. Investing in the S&P 500 would have provided you with a 4% higher CAGR, and $140,000 more in money when all was said and done. So while you could strictly invest in bonds, which would be considered very safe and does beat inflation, you would be missing out on a lot of money without incorporating stocks.

As stated, investors are aware of all this. Many years ago it was decided incorporating both stocks and bonds into a portfolio would be beneficial, and the 60/40 portfolio was born. This is where you place 60% of your portfolio in stocks, 40% in bonds, and then rebalance your portfolio throughout the year to keep that ratio. This is a portfolio touted by many financial advisors and online brokers. It provides gains which are comparable to investing in stocks, but with less volatility. Let's look at how this would play out in a chart over the last 32 years, rebalanced quarterly.

60% Stocks / 40% Bonds

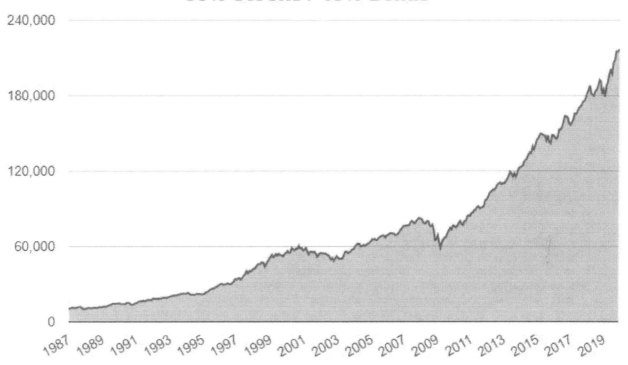

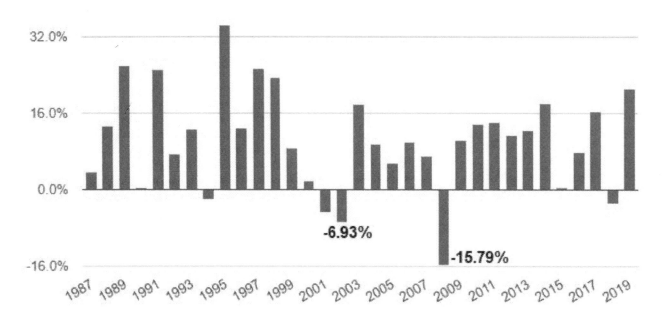

60% Stocks / 40% Bonds (Annual Returns)

-6.93%

-15.79%

<u>Stats</u>

Allocation:	60% Stocks, 40% Bonds
Initial Balance:	$10,000
Ending Balance:	$216,880
CAGR:	9.82%
Max Drawdown:	-29.05%
Worst Year:	-15.79%
Sharpe Ratio:	0.73
Sortino Ratio:	1.11

As you can see, we are doing better. This portfolio has a higher Sharpe and Sortino ratio than strictly investing in either stocks or bonds. While it doesn't have as high of gains as strictly investing in stocks, it's a much less volatile portfolio than only having stocks, with lower drawdowns throughout the years.

While this is good, what if there was a way to make this better? What if you could skew these numbers to come up with a better, more efficient portfolio? One that provides higher gains, higher Sharpe/Sortino ratios, and less drawdowns? That's exactly what I did.

As a token of appreciation to my readers, I am offering my special report titled *Crush the Market* **absolutely free!** In this report, you will learn 12 incredibly beneficial tips that will help you make money in the stock market. Just copy & paste the link below into your browser and put in your email address, and it will immediately be sent to you!

fastlink.xyz/crush

Chapter 4
The 11% Portfolio

So far we understand that both stocks and bonds have their benefits, and combining them reduces volatility. You see during good times, investors place their money in stocks, as they are more risky but provide higher returns. When the economy starts looking bleak or during bear markets, most investors rush to bonds because while they provide less returns, they are much safer than stocks and are guaranteed a return each year. That is why combining bonds with stocks reduces so much volatility with a portfolio.

As we also know, while bonds do not provide the same returns as investing in stocks, they still provide decent returns on their own, greatly beating inflation. Knowing all this I've come up with a portfolio that is able to harness both stocks and bonds, using the power of bonds to lower volatility, and the power of stocks to increase gains. Here is that portfolio.

40% Stocks / 60% Bonds

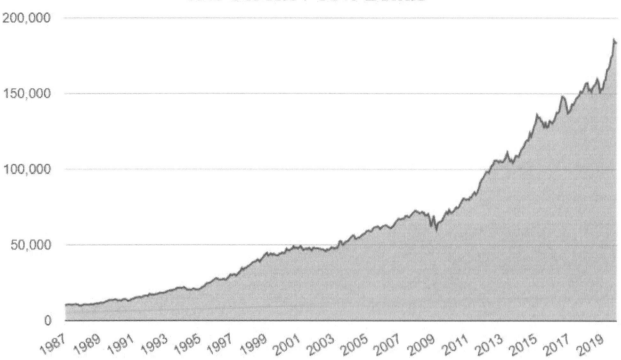

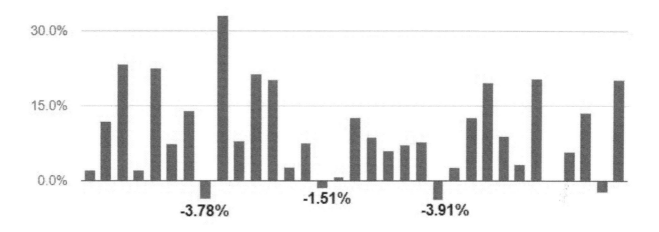

40% Stocks / 60% Bonds (Annual Returns)

Stats

Allocation:	40% Stocks, 60% Bonds
Initial Balance:	$10,000
Ending Balance:	$183,989
CAGR:	9.28%
Max Drawdown:	-16.78%
Worst Year:	-3.91%
Sharpe Ratio:	0.78
Sortino Ratio:	1.24

As you can see the CAGR for the 40/60 portfolio is comparable to the 60/40 portfolio, but with much less drawdowns and a much better "worst-year." That is what is so beneficial about this strategy! Not having to worry so much about the crashes. Let me show you this portfolio side-by-side the S&P 500 since 1987, comparing the annual returns of both. The first bar (arrow 1) is this portfolio, and the second bar (arrow 2) is the SP500.

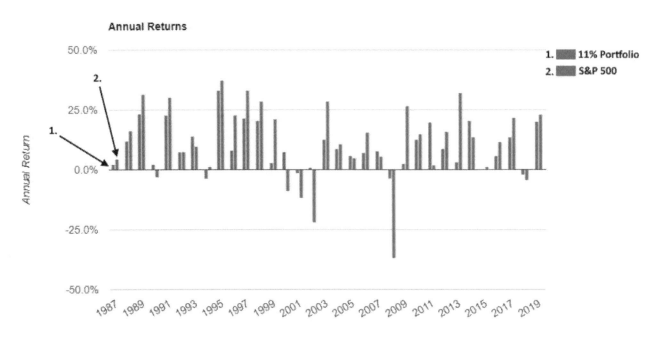

Wow! As you can tell, gains with this portfolio are comparable to the S&P 500, but the losses are greatly diminished. That is big!

Now you probably noticed the statistic displayed before which showed a "9.28% CAGR" for this portfolio allocation. You may be thinking, "I thought you said over 11%?" Let's go over how that is achieved.

The ETFs I will be advising you to buy come with dividends. As I went over in chapter 1, dividends are payments you receive quarterly from owning a stock or ETF, which is how this strategy is able to achieve an average return of over 11% annually. What's nice about having dividends associated with this strategy is no matter whether the market is up, flat, or down, you are guaranteed these dividend checks each quarter.

I've used the Vanguard mutual funds VFINX and VUSTX throughout this book. That is because they allowed me to show the history of both treasury bonds and the S&P 500 over a long term time period. ETFs did not start appearing until the 1990s.

As I explained in the first chapter though, ETFs are preferred by most investors compared to mutual funds due to their ease of use. Like mutual funds, owning ETFs come with expense ratios, however they are usually less than mutual funds.

Two common ETFs you may be familiar with are SPY (SP500) and TLT (long term treasury bonds). Let's look at the stats for these from Yahoo Finance:

SPY
Dividend Yield: 1.81%
Expense Ratio: 0.09%

TLT
Dividend Yield: 2.26%
Expense Ratio: 0.15%

With SPY, your 1.81% dividend yield is offset by the 0.09% expense ratio, leaving you with a true dividend of 1.72%. With TLT, your 2.26% dividend yield is offset by the 0.15% expense ratio, giving you a true dividend of 2.11%. Now let's go over our full income each year including the dividends we would gain from each of these ETFs.

- CAGR: 9.28%
- TLT Dividend: 2.11% * 60% = 1.27%
- SPY Dividend: 1.72% * 40% = 0.68%
- 9.28% + 1.27% + 0.68% = 11.23% yearly gain

Can we do better than this? While preparing this book, I started looking for other ETF options. I came across two ETFs, both from Vanguard, which provide better dividends and lower expense ratios. Those two ETFs are VOO (SP500) and VGLT (long term treasury bonds). Let's now look at returns using these two ETFs.

VOO	**VGLT**
Dividend Yield: 1.95%	Dividend Yield: 2.39%
Expense Ratio: 0.03%	Expense Ratio: 0.07%
True Dividend: 1.92%	True Dividend: 2.32%

Now we will make our final calculations:

- CAGR: 9.28%
- VGLT: 2.32% * 60% = 1.39%
- VOO: 1.92% * 40% = 0.77%
- 9.28% + 1.39% + 0.77% = **11.44% Yearly Returns**

And there you have it! **A portfolio consisting of 60% VGLT and 40% VOO** will provide you a yearly return of over 11%, both beating the S&P 500 average and providing you with much less volatility and drawdowns.

Something else to note is, as mentioned, the worst year for this portfolio equated to a loss of -3.91%. However, after calculating in the dividend payments you would have received (+2.16%), it actually equates to a loss of only -1.75%... that's pretty good! Compare this to annual returns of -37% for the SP500 and -13% for long term treasury bonds, and you can understand that losing -1.75% during a bad year is not too shabby!

You may have some questions related to taxes, rebalancing, etc. I have devoted the next chapter to the most common questions associated with this strategy.

Chapter 5
Questions & Answers

As stated you may have a few questions related to this strategy. I will try to go over the most common questions here.

Is there any risk with this strategy? It seems too good to be true?
There are two risks which should be taken into consideration with this strategy, though both are unlikely to occur.

The first risk would be if stocks and bonds for some reason stopped inversely correlating. As in if a crash occurred, and bonds went down along with stocks. This occurred in the United States in the 1940s and 1970s, however there were a variety of reasons for this, and both crashes recovered fairly quickly. While I can't speak for other countries, I can say this would be rather improbable in the United States. The reason why is, as I explained previously in the book, US bonds are backed by the US government. You are guaranteed the percentage amount issued on the bond, and would only not receive it if the US government went "out of business." Do I think the US government is going anywhere... no. This means when crashes occur, investors will rush to bonds because they are a "safe-haven", and will continue to be a safe-haven for the foreseeable future. If bonds and stocks however did start directly correlating, you could use the strategy I present in my book *The Crash Signal* (**fastlink.xyz/crash**) which would allow you to go into cash before the crash.

The second risk would be if runaway inflation occurred in the United States. This would most likely make the bond rate at the time, which is currently 1.75%, worthless. This is because inflation would destroy the dollar's value, and you would lose money at a greater rate than what the bond is paying. Considering the United States is currently the world's currency, has a strong economy, and a stable government that isn't socialist (yet), the chances of something like this ever happening are also rather slim. And if it ever did occur, everyone would be screwed, even people who put their money under a mattress or went into cash. Meaning unless you had all your money in Bitcoin or gold, everyone would be in the same boat you were.

The only way to avoid *all* risks associated with stocks or bonds would be to diversify your investments. As in include gold, real estate, etc. in your investment portfolio. This is a personal decision and something you may want to research more on your own.

How will negative interest rates effect this strategy?

Never before in history have countries implemented negative interest rates until 2009, when Sweden started the process and other countries have since followed suit. You see, countries lower their interest rates in an effort to boost their economies. It is something known as "quantitative easing" (QE). Someone in Sweden decided 0% wasn't low enough though, and said let's make our rates **negative**. As in if you buy a bond from the Swedish government, you end up with **less** money at the end of the year. So let's say a country had a negative 1% interest rate, and you invested $100 into a treasury bond. At the end of the year you'd have $99. Meaning just keeping your money in cash would be a better option than buying a bond. What's baffling is people are still buying bonds from countries who offer negative interest rates which makes absolutely no sense to me! Data has also shown that the negative rates do not end up helping the economy in the way they were intended to.

As of writing this book, the interest rate set by the Federal Reserve of the United States is 1.75%. However, negative interest rates could potentially come to the US. While I have no ill will towards the president, president Trump is urging the Federal Reserve chair to go to negative interest rates. The Federal Reserve is resistant and most likely will not do it. If it ever were to occur though, this actually *increases* the price of VGLT, which would be good for this strategy. Federal Reserve rates and the price of treasury ETFs like VGLT and TLT are inversely related. Meaning when the Fed lowers rates, these ETFs rise in price.

This confused me when I first learned about, but let me explain. These ETFs have exposure to bonds, meaning bonds that were already in the general market. When the Fed cuts rates, that means new bonds will pay less money. However, VGLT and TLT have older bonds which pay more money, and thus they are now worth more.

However the inverse is also true. As in if the Fed is done with quantitative easing, and now wants to implement quantitative tightening (QT), which is where they raise interest rates, these bond ETFs will now likely decrease in price. That is because the increase in interest rates makes new bonds pay more than the bonds which these ETFs are exposed to. Knowing this, it's important to keep track of what the Federal Reserve is doing with their interest rates which is usually big news on cable networks. The current Federal Reserve rate can be found on TradingEconomics.com, which I have a direct link to here: fastlink.xyz/rates. This website also displays the reserve rates from other countries as well.

What about gold or Bitcoin? Why didn't you include it in this strategy?
You could compare both gold and Bitcoin to bonds, in the fact that they are considered by some to be "safe havens," with gold of course being more mainstream than Bitcoin. The issue that I've found when looking at the history of gold is it sometimes goes up during crashes and sometimes goes down... and I don't know what will happen in the future. Let me show you an inflation adjusted chart of the 100 year history of gold. The grey vertical bars on the chart are periods when recessions were occurring.

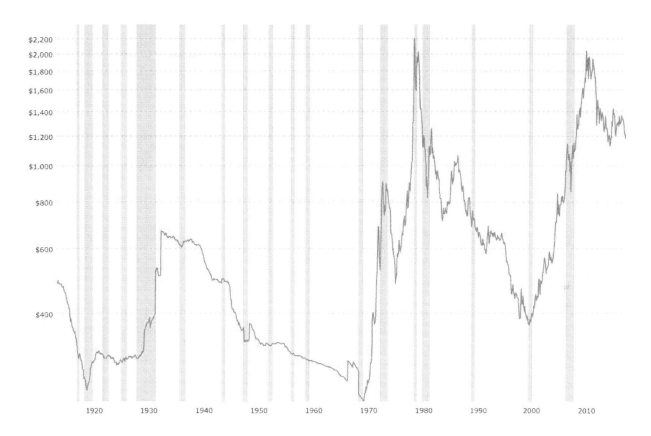

If you look at this chart, during some crashes gold went up, and during other crashes gold went down. Meaning it's essentially a crap shoot. And had you held gold since 1980, you'd still be down to this day!

Bitcoin on the other hand really doesn't have any history through crashes, so no one knows what it will do. Some speculate that it will rise, as many would use it as a safe haven, however current data shows Bitcoin correlates more with stocks than not, so I don't know if this will truly happen.

So while having some Bitcoin or gold (ticker GLD) in your portfolio may be beneficial, I didn't feel it added to this strategy, and I find both rather unreliable as safe havens.

What do you mean by "rebalance"?

When you initially implement this strategy, you will place 60% of your total account balance in VGLT, and 40% in VOO. Considering ETF prices are constantly moving, each day that goes by these percentages are getting skewed. Meaning after you initially buy these ETFs, a month later 58% of your portfolio could be in VGLT while 42% could be in VOO. These need to be "rebalanced" in order to get back to the appropriate 60/40 ratio. While rebalancing more often tends to be better, once a quarter is just fine for the average investor. Meaning you should set an alert on your phone for January 1st, April 1st, July 1st, and October 1st, as times to rebalance your portfolio. Let's go over an example with $10,000.

Let's say you invest $10,000 on January 1st using this strategy. You place $6,000 in VGLT and $4,000 in VOO. On April 1st (one quarter later), you check your account and find VGLT has remained flat while VOO is up to $4,500. This means you now have a total of $10,500 in your account. Sixty percent of $10,500 equates to $6,300. This means you need to sell $300 worth of VOO and place it in VGLT, to get back to the proper 60/40 ratio.

$10,500 * 60% = $6,300 (VGLT)
$10,500 * 40% = $4,200 (VOO)

Each quarter you will always only sell one ETF, and buy one ETF. As the amount you sell with one is the amount you will end up purchasing of the other.

How do taxes work for this strategy?

As you may be aware, there is a large difference in the amount you pay with short term versus long term capital gains taxes. These amounts differ depending on what tax bracket you are in. I have a chart below showing you these figures.

Short-Term & Long-Term Capital Gains Tax Rates By Income For Singles		
Income	Short-Term Capital Gains Tax Rate	Long-Term Capital Gains Tax Rate
Up to $9,525	10%	0%
$9,526 to $38,600	12%	0%
$38,601 to $38,700	12%	15%
$38,701 to $82,500	22%	15%
$82,501 to $157,500	24%	15%
$157,501 to $200,000	32%	15%
$200,001 to $425,800	35%	15%
$425,801 to $500,000	35%	20%
$500,001 and over	37%	20%
ST capital gains tax is a tax on profits from the sale of an asset held for <1 year		
ST capital gains tax rate = federal marginal income tax rate		
Source: IRS, FinancialSamurai.com		

You will only need to sell a small portion of one of your individual ETFs each quarter, meaning most of your funds will stay invested. And you are only paying taxes on the gains, not the amount sold. For example, let's say you have $100,000 in your brokerage account and make a $50,000 yearly salary, putting you in the 22% short term capital gains tax bracket.

On April 1st, when the first quarter ends, VGLT is up 4% ($62,400) and VOO is up 2% ($40,800). This equates to a new total of $103,200. You need to rebalance, so you sell $480 worth of VGLT to add to VOO. You then only need to pay short term capital gains on 4% (your profits) of $480, which comes out to $19.20. So you pay 22% in taxes on $19.20, meaning you only owe the government $4.22 using this strategy. Take that Uncle Sam!

And then of course when you sell any of your ETFs after a 1 year time period, you would pay the long term capital gain rate associated with your tax bracket in correlation to any profits you have made. The only exception to these rules would be if you are buying/selling these ETFs within an individual retirement account (IRA). In this case, short term capital gains do not apply because you only pay taxes when you remove the funds from the account, which most likely will only occur after you retire.

Something else to note is any losses you have incurred throughout your stock career can be deducted from the gains. Meaning you only have to start paying taxes on your gains once you are completely in the green from all your previous losses. More info on this can be found from Investopedia here: fastlink.xyz/capital.

How do I get my dividend?
Dividends are provided each quarter and deposited into your brokerage account. Many commission free brokers like Robinhood and Webull do not offer a dividend reinvestment plan (DRIP). This means the money ends up in your balance each quarter, and you need to manually use it to buy more of each ETF. If you plan on using this strategy long term and don't want the hassle, I suggest using a broker that offers

automatic dividend reinvestment. Charles Schwab and Firstrade, both commission free brokers, offer DRIP and also allow you to manage your own 401K. Meaning you could open an IRA with one of these brokers and use this strategy, which most likely will provide much larger returns than whatever your employer is currently providing you, for your retirement account. I currently have an IRA with Firstrade to manage my retirement funds. While the phone app itself is not the greatest I've ever used, it does what it's supposed to and is commission free, so I can't complain.

How do I pay the ETF expenses?
Expenses are automatically adjusted in the ETF price, and you never have to worry about paying them. All you need to know is they are associated when owning ETFs, and do very slightly offset your gains.

What if I live in another country than the United States?
You have two options if you live in a country other than the United States.

The first would be to invest in the US market with the strategy I just went over. Many brokers allow you to trade stocks from any country, however you may need to request special permissions to do so. Make sure to check with your broker to find out how. Then when you get permission, you would buy the two ETFs I went over in this book.

Your second option would be to find correlating ETFs which are available in your country, and use the same 40/60 ratio to invest in them. As in an ETF which correlates with the top companies in your country at 40% of your portfolio, and an ETF which correlates with long term treasury bonds from your country's government at 60% of your portfolio. While it of course may differ from the numbers I went over in this book, it most likely will share a similar relationship in terms of the CAGR, max drawdown, etc.

◆　◆　◆

If you are enjoying this book, could you please leave a review on Amazon? It would be greatly appreciated and allow me to come out with more informative books in the future. A shortened link to the review page is below:

fastlink.xyz/set

Conclusion

While the typical 60% stock/40% bond portfolio does have a slightly higher CAGR, the drawdowns and "worst year" are much larger. I made this book with the intention of a "set and forget" portfolio. As in corrections, crashes, etc. are not to be much of a worry, and you can leave your money in this portfolio indefinitely without needing to worry if you'll wake up to find 50% of your money missing from a crash. And considering both the Sortino and Sharpe ratios from the last 32 years, this is a better portfolio than everything else I went over in this book.

I hope I was able to provide you with useful knowledge regarding the stock market, and a strategy you can feel good about investing in for the long run. You can find more of my books by going to my website at TradeMoreStocks.com. Also, feel free to contact me if you have any questions. My email address is tim@trademorestocks.com. Enjoy!

If you enjoyed this book, you may also like:

The Green Line
Buy the Bottom of Any Stock Market Correction

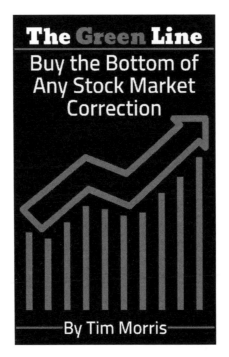

Shortened Link to Book
fastlink.xyz/green

A correction in the stock market occurs on average once a year, at a drop of 14%. What if you could capitalize on this drop by buying at the very bottom and selling at the very top? In *The Green Line*, Tim Morris shows you **how to do just that**, letting you in on a little known indicator which he has coined "The Green Line". Find out more by going to the link above.

How to Actually Day Trade for a Living
The One Book Stock Educators DO NOT Want You to Read

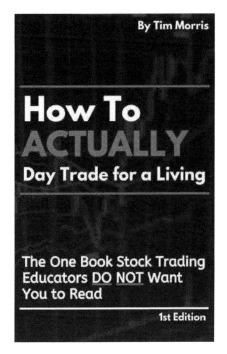

Shortened Link to Book
fastlink.xyz/day

Stock educators hate him! In this tell all book, Tim Morris gives you the raw truth about day trading. He first exposes the day trading industry, going over the deception perpetrated by the so called "professionals." He then gives traders a real look at how to day trade. He goes over the necessary software, what a typical day entails, and even **8 strategies** you can immediately start using to day trade. Find out more at the link above!

The 5 Minute Swing Trade
*A Simple Stock Market Swing Trading Strategy that Takes 5
Minutes to Research & Actually Works!*

Shortened Link to Book
fastlink.xyz/swing

Finally! A swing trading strategy that **actually works!** In *The 5 Minute Swing Trade*,
Tim Morris goes over a swing trading strategy which takes just 5 minutes to research,
and a win rate that would make Warren Buffett jealous. Tim then explains the
mechanics behind the trade, and the reasons it works so well. Find out more!

The Crash Signal

The One Signal that Predicts a Stock Market Crash

Shortened Link to Book
fastlink.xyz/crash

Stock market crashes are inevitable, but losing money doesn't have to be! In this ground breaking book, Tim Morris exposes **the one signal** that has flashed before every stock market crash for the last 60 years. He then tells you the **exact point** to get out to avoid the crash, & even how to make money while it's happening! Save yourself from the next crash with *The Crash Signal*!

Made in the USA
San Bernardino, CA
09 February 2020